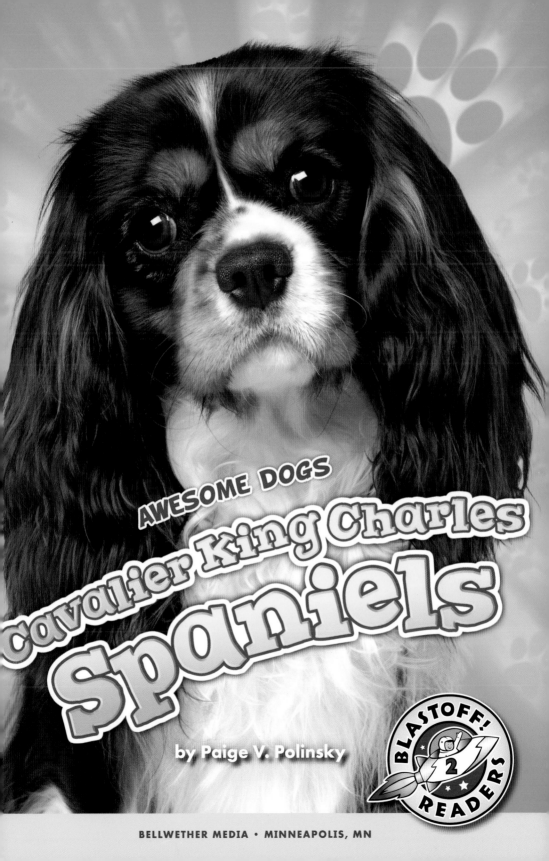

AWESOME DOGS

Cavalier King Charles Spaniels

by Paige V. Polinsky

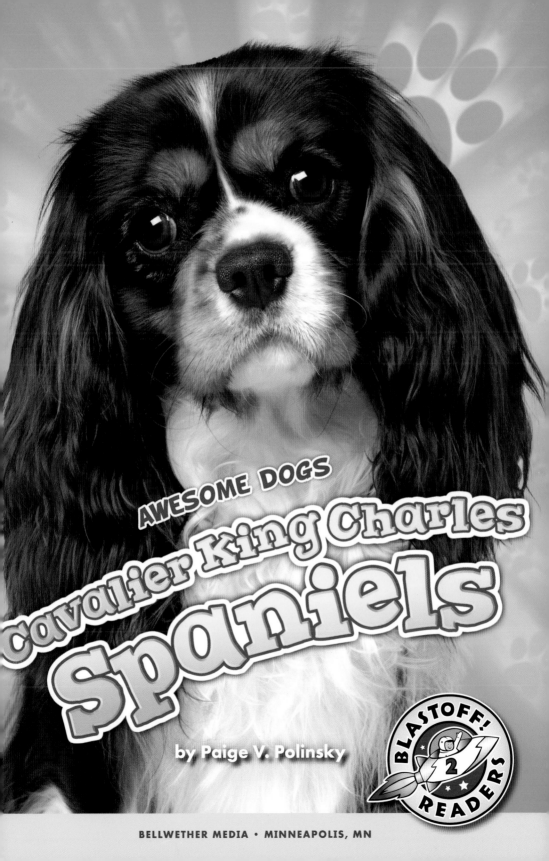

BLASTOFF! READERS

BELLWETHER MEDIA • MINNEAPOLIS, MN

Note to Librarians, Teachers, and Parents:

Blastoff! Readers are carefully developed by literacy experts and combine standards-based content with developmentally appropriate text.

Level 1 provides the most support through repetition of high-frequency words, light text, predictable sentence patterns, and strong visual support.

Level 2 offers early readers a bit more challenge through varied simple sentences, increased text load, and less repetition of high-frequency words.

Level 3 advances early-fluent readers toward fluency through increased text and concept load, less reliance on visuals, longer sentences, and more literary language.

Level 4 builds reading stamina by providing more text per page, increased use of punctuation, greater variation in sentence patterns, and increasingly challenging vocabulary.

Level 5 encourages children to move from "learning to read" to "reading to learn" by providing even more text, varied writing styles, and less familiar topics.

Whichever book is right for your reader, Blastoff! Readers are the perfect books to build confidence and encourage a love of reading that will last a lifetime!

This edition first published in 2018 by Bellwether Media, Inc.

No part of this publication may be reproduced in whole or in part without written permission of the publisher. For information regarding permission, write to Bellwether Media, Inc., Attention: Permissions Department, 5357 Penn Avenue South, Minneapolis, MN 55419.

Library of Congress Cataloging-in-Publication Data

Names: Polinsky, Paige V., author.
Title: Cavalier King Charles Spaniels / by Paige V. Polinsky.
Other titles: Blastoff! Readers. 2, Awesome Dogs.
Description: Minneapolis, MN : Bellwether Media, Inc., [2018] | Series: Blastoff! Readers: Awesome Dogs | Audience: Ages 5-8. | Audience: K to Grade 3. | Includes bibliographical references and index.
Identifiers: LCCN 2017028767 | ISBN 9781626177413 (hardcover : alk. paper) | ISBN 9781681034560 (ebook)
Subjects: LCSH: Cavalier King Charles spaniel–Juvenile literature.
Classification: LCC SF429.C36 P65 2018 | DDC 636.752/4–dc23
LC record available at https://lccn.loc.gov/2017028767

Editor: Betsy Rathburn   Designer: Lois Stanfield

Printed in the United States of America, North Mankato, MN.

Table of Contents

What Are Cavalier King Charles Spaniels?

Cavalier King Charles spaniels are small dogs. They are known for their large, round eyes.

These dogs are also called Cavs.

Cavs are one of the largest **breeds** in the **Toy Group** of the **American Kennel Club**.

They can weigh up to
18 pounds (8 kilograms).

Feathered Fur

black, white, and tan

Cavs have soft, **feathered** fur. Their **coats** are often black, white, and tan.

Cavalier King Charles Spaniel Coats

Blenheim   ruby   black and tan

They can be **Blenheim** or **ruby**, too. Black and tan Cavs are also common.

Cavs have short **muzzles** with black noses.

Cavalier King Charles Spaniel Profile

flat head

large eyes

feathered fur

Life Span: 9 to 15 years

Trainability:

1   2   3   4   5   6

Hardest to train   Easiest to train

Their long ears sit high on their heads. This makes their heads look flat!

History of Cavalier King Charles Spaniels

Cavs began in England. They come from toy spaniels used as **royal** lapdogs in the late 1600s.

England

N
W E
S

young Charles II with
his siblings

King Charles I and his son
Charles II loved these dogs.

When King Charles II passed away, the dogs became less popular. They were **bred** to have smaller heads and shorter noses.

The new dogs were called
King Charles spaniels.

In the early 1900s, an American named Roswell Eldridge **revived** the dogs' early looks.

The old breed was back! These dogs became Cavalier King Charles spaniels.

Sweet Spaniels

Cavs are very sweet. They love meeting new people.

These **affectionate** dogs are
also gentle. They make great
therapy dogs.

These dogs can be playful,
too. They like to learn
new tricks.

Most of all, Cavs love to snuggle!

Glossary

affectionate—loving

American Kennel Club—an organization that keeps track of dog breeds in the United States

Blenheim—a coat color of solid white with reddish brown markings

bred—purposely mated two dogs to make puppies with certain qualities

breeds—types of dogs

coats—the hair or fur covering some animals

feathered—longer on the ears, legs, or tail

muzzles—the noses and mouths of some animals

revived—brought back interest in something or brought it back into use

royal—related to kings and queens

ruby—a dark reddish brown color

therapy dogs—dogs that comfort people who are sick, hurt, or have a disability

Toy Group—a group of the smallest dog breeds; most dogs in the Toy Group were bred to be companions.

To Learn More

AT THE LIBRARY

Gagne, Tammy. *Chihuahuas, Pomeranians, and Other Toy Dogs.* North Mankato, Minn.: Capstone Press, 2017.

Johnson, Jinny. *Cavalier King Charles Spaniel.* Mankato, Minn.: Smart Apple Media, 2015.

Schuetz, Kari. *Pugs.* Minneapolis, Minn.: Bellwether Media, 2017.

ON THE WEB

Learning more about Cavalier King Charles spaniels is as easy as 1, 2, 3.

1. Go to www.factsurfer.com.

2. Enter "Cavalier King Charles spaniels" into the search box.

3. Click the "Surf" button and you will see a list of related web sites.

With factsurfer.com, finding more information is just a click away.

Index

The images in this book are reproduced through the courtesy of: Eric Isselee, front cover, pp. 4, 9 (center, right), 12; Lenkadan, pp. 4-5; Sergey Ryumin/ Getty Images, pp. 6-7; Mikkel Bigandt, p. 7; Fotyma, pp. 8-9; otsphoto, p. 9 (left); Jan Wilusz/ EyeEm/ Getty Images, p. 10; kuban_girl, p. 11; Wikipedia, pp. 12-13; Waldemar Dabrowski, pp. 14-15; Nancy Dressel, p. 15; Juniors Bildarchiv GmbH/ Alamy, p. 16; Morrison Media, pp. 16-17; Julie Campbell, p. 18; Petra Wegner/ Alamy, p. 19; Martin Mehes, p. 20; cynoclub, p. 21.